Public Relations Planning, Research, and Measurement

Mark Hunter LaVigne
Colin Babiuk

Rock's Mills Press
Rock's Mills, Ontario • Oakville, Ontario
2024

Published by

Rock's Mills Press
www.rocksmillspress.com

For information about this title, including retail, adoption, and bulk orders as well as permissions requests, please contact the publisher at customer.service@rocksmillspress.com.

Contents

You cannot plan without research and measurement.
You cannot measure without a plan.
—Mark Hunter LaVigne

Foreword
Why You Should Think Before Saying "Yes"
Daniel Granger

Every day, both young and seasoned communication and public relations professionals are asked to write and issue press releases. Before you say yes to such a request, you must do some research because a message sent without research is most likely not very valuable to the organization and not of much interest to its publics. Public communication is a process that's effective only when a specific and comprehensive process is followed. When you're asked to draft a press release, you need to take the time to truly understand the issue, know who is involved, establish what you want to accomplish, who must be reached, when and how, and determine how you will measure the outcome. Thoroughly researching quantitative and qualitative data and measuring results properly are two essential pillars of any meaningful and effective communication process.

This book is a communication planning toolkit, developed by Mark Hunter LaVigne, MA, APR, FCPRS, LM, a senior PR professional and popular instructor at several Toronto area colleges, and Colin Babiuk, MA, APR, FCPRS, Associate Professor and Public Relations Program Coordinator at MacEwan University in Edmonton.

The authors unpack RACE—the process recognized and taught as the gold standard in communication by the Canadian Public Relations Society (CPRS), the Public Relations Society of America (PRSA) and the International Association of Business Communicators (IABC)—in a clear, direct and concise manner with the help of two outstanding professionals and former CPRS National Presidents, Kim Blanchette, APR, Chart.PR (CIPR), FCPRS and Colleen Killingsworth, MCM, APR, FCPRS.

In this book, you'll find all the elements that need to come together to develop a proper communication plan, from research to outcome assessment. Your employers and clients alike deserve this exercise on your part before you recommend and implement a tactic. Even though they are often short on time and ask you for a one-pager and specific actions, this planning is key both for you and for your credibility.

Happy reading!

—Daniel Granger, C.M., APR, FCPRS

Introduction

This book was created to assist entry-level communicators in learning how to develop successful campaigns, as well as to provide more seasoned practitioners with a refresher on the elements of an effective communication plan.

Organizations face many challenges in their pursuit to conduct business—from a change in regulations that may impact normal operations, to pushback from a public interest group that has concerns with how the organization conducts business. In all cases, the organization must communicate its position to its publics in an attempt to create a shared understanding and ensure mutual benefit.

A communication plan is written to help guide a communicator and their employer or client through the process of identifying and resolving an issue, or taking advantage of an opportunity, through the use of communication. The effectiveness of a communication plan depends to a large extent on the input from the employer or the client as well as on the skills of the communication professional. Such a professional is familiar with techniques used to influence public attitudes and opinions. The key word here is *communication*.

As communicators, we provide a service to different departments within an organization to create awareness and understanding of its programs and initiatives. Typically, we do not own the project, but we are an essential partner in recommending a course of action based on our research into target audiences—their needs, their perceptions and beliefs about the project, and how they may react to the project.

Communication plans are strategic, living documents, meaning that they can change depending on changing circumstances. Because of this, we must continuously monitor the situation we are following to not only identify any changes, but to assess what these changes mean both in the short term and in the more distant future.

What Does a Communication Plan Do?

A plan serves as a guide for a communicator on how to obtain background information about an issue, how the issue does impact, and could potentially impact, the relationships between the organization and its publics, how the issue aligns with the organization's values and principles, and why it is important to communicate to these audiences to increase both awareness and understanding of the issue.

A communication plan also provides the information required by senior management to fully understand the issue, and the real and perceived threats or benefits of the situation. They can then make informed decisions based on this information. The plan lays out how communication will be used to meet the plan's goals, which could include managing an issue, building support from the community, or improving engagement with employees. Based on this gathering of information, a communication plan provides the communicator and senior management with a strategic roadmap to address the situation.

Communication plans can:

- Get people to do something;
- Get people NOT to do something;
- Influence ideas and behaviours; and
- Help to win the consent of publics so an organization can carry out a particular action.

Plans are written to:

- Help or increase stakeholder or staff support;
- Resolve an issue limiting the organization in realizing its mission or a situation offering a potential advantage to the organization or its publics;
- Communicate a change in policy or procedure; and
- Convey a new direction or positioning.

A plan's effectiveness can be measured by conducting an ongoing critical examination of the communication goals and

Effective communications planning is a vital ingredient in ensuring overall organizational success, regardless of the size of the organization or the nature of its activities.

objectives and their success, and pinpointing where the operation has not achieved its full potential.

Communication plans serve to:

- Identify and clarify an issue;
- Identify relevant audiences and publics;
- Create an understanding of audience and public perceptions and needs;
- Establish appropriate messages;
- Ensure consistent messaging; and
- Develop tools, tactics and methods for getting the message to audiences and publics effectively.

Communication plans can be used to develop a case study report when campaign elements, results and post mortems analyses are added after execution. Plans are easily adaptable into a case study, which preserves the work, informs future work and can be adapted for an award entry should the campaign resonate particularly well.

Communication Plan Template

While the organization you work or study with will likely have its own communication plan template, we suggest such a template include the following elements:

- Background
- Research
- Analysis/Assessment
- Goals
- Objectives
- Target Audiences
- Key Messages
- Strategies
- Tactics
- Timelines
- Budget
- Human Capital
- Evaluation

You will see that communication plans include research and evaluation. **Research** assists in determining the scope of the issue, the public perception and beliefs around the issue, and the appropriate audience with whom to communicate. **Evaluation** provides an ongoing critical examination of the communication goals and objectives and their success. Research and evaluation are essential components in developing an effective communication plan.

The headings in this book differ slightly from those provided by our esteemed guest authors Blanchette and Killingsworth. Our headings are intended to provide a paradigm for PR educators and practitioners. The good work by our guest authors is laser-focused on providing RACE (Research, Analysis, Communication, Evaluation) executive summaries, particularly for CPRS and PRSA case studies, award entries and APR case samples.

The table below provides a visual guide to how each section of a communication plan falls into one of the elements of RACE:

Activity	Heading	RACE
—	Background	—
Research	Research	R
Research	Analysis	A
Research	Goals	A
Research and Measurement	Objectives	C
Research	Target audiences	C
Research	Key Messages	C
	Strategy	C
Research and Measurement	Tactics	C
Measurement	Timelines	C
Research and Measurement	Budget	E
Measurement	Human Capital	E
Measurement	Awareness[1]	E
Measurement	Acceptance[2]	E
Measurement	Action[3]	E

1. **Awareness** deals with levels of information, understanding and retention. For instance, have the right messages been used with the right tools for the right publics?

2. **Acceptance** deals with levels of interest or attitude. For instance, did we make sure that our key publics paid attention to and remembered our messages?

3. **Action with opinion** (verbal action) or **behaviour** (physical action).

Executive Summaries:
The RACE Formula

Kim Blanchette, APR, Chart.PR, FCPRS
and Colleen Killingsworth, MCM, APR, FCPRS

Ultimately, organizations are seeking relationships with their stakeholders, consumers, employees and the public. If you want a strong, mutually beneficial relationship with those around you, you must adopt a process of communication planning that supports symmetrical communication. As described in James Grunig's *Excellence Theory*, **symmetrical communication** is the process of ensuring decisions made by an organization are mutually beneficial for both the organization itself and its audiences.

Articulated by John E. Marston in 1963 in *The Nature of Public Relations*, the **RACE formula** (research, action, communication and evaluation) is an in-depth and evaluative communication planning process encompassing four phases: **Research**, **Action and Planning**, **Communication and Relationship Building**, and **Evaluation**.

(See the next page for a representation of the RACE formula in graphic form.)

The RACE formula is the communications planning process endorsed by the Canadian Public Relations Society (CPRS), the Public Relations Society of America (PRSA) and the International Association of Business Communicators (IABC).

According to the Canadian Public Relations Society (2017), "Before launching an effective public relations program, you must understand an organization's environment—especially the prevailing attitudes and issues as they are perceived by employees, shareholders and residents of the community or communities in which a program will run."

There's a lot on the line. In fact, in a study conducted by Leger for the CPRS in 2021, 87 percent of Canadians surveyed reported that the work of public relations and communications professionals played an important role in helping manage the speed and volume of information while 80 percent agreed on the importance of the role that communicators play in organizations with a strong emphasis on ethics and professional standards.

This reality calls on public relations and communications professionals to ensure that the advice and counsel they provide to organizations is founded in the principles adopted by CPRS and other professional organizations; that we are able to provide evidence for our insights and advice; and that we are ultimately able to help organizations deliver on their vision, mandate and business objectives through strategic communications programs rooted in the RACE formula.

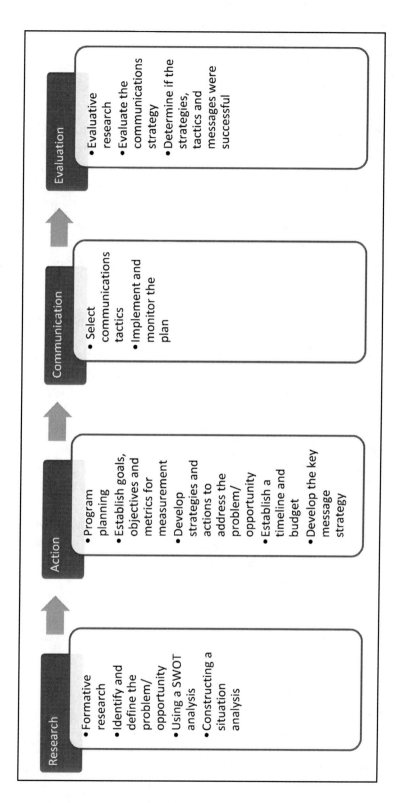

Research
- Formative research
- Identify and define the problem/opportunity
- Using a SWOT analysis
- Constructing a situation analysis

Action
- Program planning
- Establish goals, objectives and metrics for measurement
- Develop strategies and actions to address the problem/opportunity
- Establish a timeline and budget
- Develop the key message strategy

Communication
- Select communications tactics
- Implement and monitor the plan

Evaluation
- Evaluative research
- Evaluate the communications strategy
- Determine if the strategies, tactics and messages were successful

Both an Art and a Science

At its core, the RACE formula is three-quarters science and one-quarter art. It's the science behind communication planning that helps to build credibility as communicators. More than ever, leaders are demanding communicators back up their plans and recommendations with data and analysis. Gone are the days when you could respond with "I think we should do this." Today's leaders seek the data that drives insights and the metrics that prove results.

Let's take a closer look at the science behind the RACE formula—research, analysis, communication and evaluation.

Both formative and evaluative research use formal and informal, qualitative and quantitative research methods.

Formative research focuses on gathering insights from internal and external stakeholders to define the problem or opportunity. A good starting point is understanding what one's own or other organizations have done in the past under similar circumstances. The outcome of such research provides the communicator with the data and information required to complete a comprehensive situation analysis to help better understand priority publics, set communications goals, SMART objectives and metrics for measurement, and develop key messages.

Evaluative research assesses campaign results by using the metrics for measuring objectives to gather the data and information required to determine the overall success of communications efforts. With evaluative data and analysis in hand, the communicator will be able to report the overall return on investment to the organization's leadership.

Research and evaluation become a cycle, with evaluative research often indicating what needs to be done next and forming the basis of the next round of formative research.

Now let's look at the art behind the RACE formula—action and communication.

The art behind the RACE formula lies in applying the analysis gained through your research to plan a communication campaign and determine what communications tactics and channels will be used to support two-way symmetrical communication with an organization's publics. Ethical, transparent and factual public relations are critical to building trust and relationships with your publics. It's not enough to just send messages anymore; there needs to be an ongoing conversation between an organization and its publics.

On Organizational Listening

In his book *Organizational Listening: This Missing Essential in Public Communication* (2016a) Jim Macnamara describes **organizational listening** as encompassing the "culture, policies, structure, processes, resources, skills, technologies, and practices applied by an organization to give recognition, acknowledgement, attention, interpretation, understanding, consideration, and response to its stakeholders and publics."

Organizational listening is more than interpersonal relationships and being respectful of others. Organizations today have broad, diverse, and complex audience and stakeholder groups that may include hundreds of thousands, if not millions, of people over a large geographic area. These organizations must be willing and able to listen to very diverse and large groups of customers, members, patients, students, citizens, regulated and non-regulated entities, and employees. We are quite good at speaking. But talking on its own does not constitute communication (Macnamara, 2016b). In other words, communication is a *dialogue* that requires openness between both parties. It requires both speaking and listening.

To ensure that you are providing your organization with effective communications, all four steps of the RACE process should be followed and continuously monitored. The best results come from ongoing data gathering and analysis, which helps you to focus on the most effective strategies to build relationships with your audiences.

Given the fact that organizations today work with broad, diverse, and complex groups of stakeholders and audience members, it's important that they develop the ability to listen carefully and comprehensively to what those stakeholders andaudiences are telling them, rather than regarding communication as only from the organization outward.

Plan on a Page:
Providing an Executive Summary for Busy Decision-Makers

You've spent months on your organization's latest communication strategy. You've done your research and analysis, developed audience personas, identified risks and mitigation, and developed goals and objectives that align with the organization's goals. Your tactics are strategic, ladder up to your objectives, and you've got the timeline, budget and evaluation plan articulated in detail. You're proud of the 52-page plan you've submitted to your executive, demonstrating how communications will deliver tangible results for your organization and build reputational equity.

Being able to distill your communications plan into a one-page executive summary is a skill that public relations practitioners must develop in order to be effective in today's fast-moving business environment. Nor is this a new idea. In 1940, British prime minister Winston Churchill sent a memo entitled "Brevity" to the members of his War Cabinet. "The discipline of setting out the real points concisely," he observed, "will prove an aid to clearer thinking."

Then you get a call from the CEO's office asking if you can provide a one-page summary of your plan so the executive can take a quick scan and decide on the next steps. Impossible, you think. Perhaps even a bit insulting. After all, this is an in-depth strategy backed by extensive research and insightful analysis. Alas, it happens to us all. There are ways to build that all-important executive summary that demonstrate how RACE was applied to this particular communications requirement, get executive buy-in and highlight the extent of the work conducted.

First, don't lose the opportunity to educate. Explain RACE and how it was applied to the plan's development. Use the flow of RACE to outline your plan on a page and focus on what's in it for the organization and its vision or mandate. Here's a quick outline for your one-page executive summary.

- **Introduction**—the problem or opportunity you are addressing in one sentence.
- **Method**—explanation of RACE, what it is and why it is important.
- **Research**—two to three bullets of the formative research conducted (survey, literature review, focus groups, etc.). What is the top insight? For example, perhaps you need to increase confidence in your organization. Your research indicated that awareness of the organization alone did not contribute to higher confidence scores; however, you did find media recall of specific campaigns in the previous year was related to higher awareness and higher confidence scores. There's much research to get to that point, but you could have it as your primary research finding:

  Our top insight was that adults aged 24–65 who could recall a recent campaign from our organization had higher awareness, positive sentiment and confidence scores, suggesting that these campaigns have a direct impact on our objective to improve stakeholder confidence.

- **Analysis**—What are the organization's strengths (2–4), weaknesses (2–4), opportunities (2–4) and threats (2–4)? Usually, the analysis focuses on three aspects of the organization: its **internal environment**, its **public perception** and its **external environment**.
- **Goals and Objectives**—Use a table format to ensure your goals and objectives are clear, SMART and directly linked to your organization's vision.
- **Communications**—This can be very challenging to shorten; here, pick your top 3–5 tactics and why they will deliver on the goals and objectives. You can mention that there are other supporting tactics in the plan, but ensure you are focusing on the most impactful and those that have a resource request attached to them.
- **Timeline**—When can the executive expect to see results (don't forget to indicate when you need resources or approval of the plan to avoid being held to an unreasonable deadline after weeks or months of waiting for approval)?
- **Budget**—What is your total budget and human resource ask?
- **Evaluation**—How will you measure success? Provide 2–3 bullets.

If you've done your due diligence and created a communications plan using the RACE formula, the executive summary is not as difficult to draft as one might think. In fact, the exercise of drafting the executive summary may even identify gaps in your planning that might need to be addressed.

Using the RACE formula consistently, ensuring you understand your organization's vision, mandate, goals and objectives, and being able to distill your recommendations into a succinct one-page document are skills that hone our craft, demonstrate the value of strategic public relations advice and counsel, and build better relationships between organizations and their publics.

Background

The **background section** is a comprehensive yet concise section that provides historical context and fixes the plan in time and space. It explains the background of the situation in relation to the mission, vision, and values of the organization. It illustrates the connection between the current situation and its alignment with the organization. How does this situation limit the organization in realizing its mission? How does it support or conflict with the organization's history, values, and/or mission? How does the issue offer a potential advantage to the organization or its publics? How does the issue affect the visibility and/or reputation of the organization?

A paragraph or two will suffice. For example:

> BestHomes is an established family-owned home builder with a 25-year history. BestHomes is known as a luxury home builder that pays attention to the little things and for adding unique features that increase the desirability of these homes, such as hidden television systems and windows that self-darken for privacy. BestHomes units start at $900,000. The company has a loyal following of satisfied owners, and many wealthy people seek out a BestHomes unit for their next home purchase.
>
> Wanting to give back to the community, BestHomes is proposing a 30-unit low-income housing project to help address the rising numbers of residents unable to afford housing. The location of the project is close to an affluent community. This is the only space of land available for a project of this size.
>
> The target market for these units is working individuals and couples with lower incomes, in particular recent graduates, young couples, and new Canadians.
>
> There has been a great deal of pushback from local residents. They believe a low-income project will bring "undesirables" into their community. They are concerned that the project will lower their property values and will lead to increased criminal activity and personal safety issues.
>
> The last step in obtaining a development permit is a public open house. The approval of the building permit relies on demonstrated support from the community.

Research

In many public relations issues, there is a difference between public perception and opinion and what is actually occurring. We also see pushback on projects due to what people perceive will occur, whether or not this is true.

In any situation, we need to fully understand if an issue or opportunity is indeed actually occurring, as well as to determine the publics involved, their opinions, beliefs, and perceptions, where the publics are located, and the best media to use to connect with them. Research results will accurately identify the issue that we are trying to resolve, saving the organization time and money.

GERD ALTMANN/PIXABAY

Research is essential to the success of campaigns. One must be able to assess any change in public sentiment before and after communicating messages. Baseline research provides us with the metrics we will use in both setting objectives and measuring the overall success of a campaign. For example, if we find that 20 percent of residents approve of a project, what level of increase is achievable through communication, and how long will it take to reach that number?

Public relations works with both qualitative and quantitative measurements. **Quantitative measurement** deals with numbers and percentages. It helps to specify and determine the number of incidences. It provides the hard numbers: the figures and the statistics we will use to determine success.

Qualitative measurement is exploratory in nature. It seeks to help us understand the "whys"—why people feel a certain way or have a certain belief, thus providing insight into the issue.

Quantitative research makes use of numbers, percentages, and "hard" data. The informatuion may be gathered by the organization itself or obtained from third parties, including government agencies like Statistics Canada or companies that carry out consumer research.

Quantitative research is **formal research** in that it is structured and relies on representative data. By **representative**, we mean that the number of people participating in the research is large enough that every member of the targeted population has an equal chance of being selected for the sample. Participants are selected randomly to ensure that no one group is over or underrepresented. Results from a representative survey can be generalized to a total population; if everyone in the population were surveyed, the results would be very similar to the results of the smaller sample group.

Qualitative measurement is **informal** in nature. There may be little to no formal structure in how data is obtained and the number of people approached may be very small. Participants are not chosen randomly. In many cases, specific individuals are asked to participate. The results can not be generalized to a total population.

Qualitative research is informal, and may include individual and group interviews. Often qualitative research can help refine the nature of questions that will be asked using quantitative research tools like surveys.

To determine the direction of the questions for a survey, we can make use of **non-representative research methods,** such as focus groups. A **focus group** is not representative as not everyone in the population has a chance of participating. Instead, researchers bring together small groups of people to find out their views and opinions on a topic. Focus groups are exploratory and qualitative in nature—focusing on the emotional side of the equation rather than the hard numbers. However, the results of a focus group can be very useful in determining the questions that are asked in a formal survey.

Research can demonstrate the success of campaigns designed to change behaviour. For example, a recycling group measured PR campaign efficacy by surveying users once a year to gauge uptake and understanding of what materials could be recycled at that time. If "the needle moved" in the right direction every year (increased recycling levels, increased participation, and increased understanding by the general public in those catchment areas) then the annual communications campaign was determined a success.

What we learn up to the end of this stage will inform the development of the rest of the plan.

Consider the example of the housing development that we discussed earlier.

A formal, representative survey was conducted across the city to determine the overall level of awareness of, and degree of support for, the project.

The survey revealed that 90 per cent of those surveyed were aware of the project and 85 percent approved of the project. However, the awareness rate rose to 100 percent and the approval rate dropped to just 20 percent in the neighbourhoods adjacent to the development.

Those who were most supportive were younger adults, couples starting families, and new Canadians. Those opposed to the project were primarily older, educated, and wealthy individuals. People were more supportive of the project the further away they lived from where it would be located.

Reasons for supporting the project included a desire for affordable housing in the city, a sense of civic pride in addressing the housing crisis, and a belief that members of a community take care of each other.

The main reasons cited for not supporting the project were a belief that the project will attract undesirable residents, leading to a drop in property values and an increase in criminal activity and personal assaults.

Analysis/Assessment

Also known as a **situation analysis,** this is the stage where the research comes to life. The analysis will guide the next steps of the plan by providing insight into the publics that are impacted or have an interest, identifying their concerns or interests, and determining the degree of knowledge, understanding, and support the publics have around the issue. Based on this, the analysis will help you develop the best messages for these publics and choose the most effective medium to distribute these messages.

This section provides a synopsis of the communication plan. It is usually written at the beginning of the plan and then revisited once the plan has been written to ensure all the tactics and overall schedule and budget are accurate and match what has been set out in detail elsewhere in the plan. In essence, it is an executive summary.

If an organization's CEO has to approve a communications plan but only has five minutes to read it on the way to a meeting, this section should provide them with all the information they need to know.

The analysis section provides:

- A description of the issue;
- The history of the issue; and
- The cause of the issue.

It also sets out:

- The publics involved in the issue;
- The real and potential impacts on the organization and on the involved publics;
- How the issue will be addressed and resolved through communication; and
- The expected results of the communication plan.

This section answers the following questions:

- Who are we?
- What do we do?
- Who do we do it for?
- What are our values?
- What are the factors that led to the current situation?
- What did the research reveal?
- Who are our audiences?

- Who are we impacting, and how?
- Who has an impact on us, and how?
- What relationships are in tension?
- What are the audience's perceptions of the issue? Of us?
- What messages are required by whom?
- What is the best way to communicate with these audiences?
- What are we going to do to resolve the issue?
- How are we going to do this through communication?
- What are the expected results?

SWOT Analysis

PR professionals do not create communication plans in isolation. An **environmental scan** reveals how internal and external events can influence and impact an issue. While the situation analysis speaks to the research that identified and verified the issue, a **SWOT analysis** provides insight into the issue. SWOT stands for:

- Strengths
- Weaknesses
- Opportunities
- Threats

Business schools teach that strengths and weaknesses are internal, and that threats and opportunities are external to the organization. In communications, we view strengths and weaknesses as factors that are *currently* occurring and threats and opportunities as factors that are *likely to occur in the future* such as pending legislation or litigation. From this point of view, strengths, weaknesses, opportunities and threats can be both internal and external to an organization.

HELPFUL
TO ACHIEVING THE OBJECTIVE

HARMFUL
TO ACHIEVING THE OBJECTIVE

STRENGTHS

WEAKNESSES

OPPORTUNITIES

THREATS

RMP GRAPHICS DEPARTMENT

Returning to the example of the proposed housing development, here is a SWOT analysis for that proposed project:

Strengths	Weaknesses
• Company has a 25-year history of building quality homes. • BestHomes has a stellar safety history. • The majority of city residents believe low-income housing is needed.	• The majority of city residents don't want low-income housing close to where they live. • There is misunderstanding of the difference between low-income individuals and homeless individuals.
Threats	Opportunities

• Residents believe:
  o The development will cause crime rates to increase;
  o "Undesirable" individuals will move into the area; and
  o The community will not be safe.
	• Residents will be more supportive if they know whom the units are intended for.
	• Social and peer pressure may soften opposition.
	• Municipal and provincial government support for the project may decrease residents' resistance.

PEST
A **PEST review** identifies potential factors in the following areas:

- Political factors
- Economic issues
- Societal factors
- Technological considerations

PESTLE
A **PESTLE review** adds legal and environmental factors to the list.

- Political factors
- Economic issues
- Societal factors
- Technological considerations
- Legal issues
- Environmental issues

POLITICAL

ECONOMIC

SOCIETAL

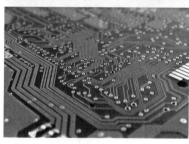

TECHNO-LOGICAL

A **PEST analysis** takes into account the factors listed above. A **PESTLE analysis** adds the two additional factors noted below.

LEGAL   **E**NVIRONMENTAL

The decision to use PEST or PESTLE would depend on whether there are legal and environmental factors involved in the issue or opportunity at hand.

Using our example of the BestHomes housing development:

Political	• City may be viewed as putting profit before people if the project is cancelled. • Reducing homelessness is a priority for the municipal and provincial governments. They will be in favor of, and can lend support to, the project.
Economic	• Risk of loss of property taxes to municipality. • Decreased profits for local businesses from purchases by new residents, since they will not be as well off as the city's traditional population. • Loss of future home sales or development contracts for BestHomes, because of anger over their taking on this project. • Loss of profits for BestHomes because of cancellation of the project.
Societal	• Housing affordability is seen as a pressing social issue that needs to be addressed. • Providing affordable housing is seen as a political priority.
Technological	Not applicable.
Legal	• Potential lawsuits from unhappy current residents if the project goes ahead.
Environmental	Not applicable.

Goal

The **goal** of a communication plan is a statement rooted in an organization's mission or vision, acknowledging an issue and sketching out how the organization hopes to see it settled. Communication goals are related to three types of situations: ones involving **reputation**, ones involving **relationships**, and ones involving **tasks**.

A **reputation goal** deals with an organization's identity and perception (for instance, improving a company's reputation within its industry). A **relationship goal** is focused on how an organization connects with its publics (for example, enhancing the relationship between a company and its customers). And a **task goal** is centered on getting certain things accomplished (for instance, increasing public support for organizational goals).

Keep in mind that we need to focus the goals on what we can resolve through **communication** as opposed to **operational goals or activities**. It also helps to think of the goal as the business goal. If we have a business problem, what is the intended outcome?

Returning again to BestHomes' proposed development, the overall goal is to build the project. This will only be possible if BestHomes can garner the support required to obtain the building permit.

Winning approval will depend on changing the beliefs and perceptions of those opposing the project. How to accomplish this will become the communication plan's objectives.

Objectives

The next step in a communication plan is to establish objectives. **Objectives** are statements emerging from an organization goal (a goal can generate many objectives), presented in clear and **measurable** terms, pointing toward particular levels of awareness, acceptance or action.

Objectives set the hard metrics that will be used to evaluate the success of a campaign. As such, objectives outline what you expect to achieve. They are audience specific. They have clear and measurable targets and always include a deadline.

Think in terms of creating **SMART objectives**, which meet key criteria:

Specific: They clearly describe a desired outcome.

Measurable: They are verifiable, identifying criteria for measurement and success.

Achievable: They may be challenging but are within the organization's range of influence.

Relevant: They contribute to broader efforts in a meaningful way.

Time-framed: The objectives include a completion timeline or date.

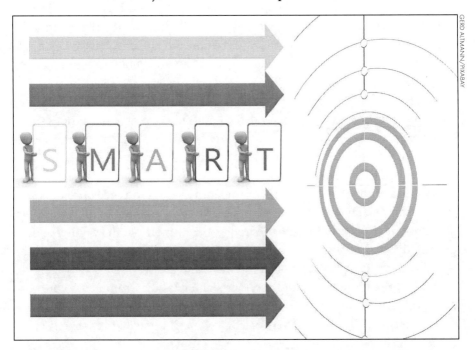

Well-thought-out objectives must have measurement built in. Measurable objectives should:

- Be specific and quantifiable and state the desired outcome;
- Include a target audience;
- Be practical;
- Refer to *ends* not *means*;
- Include a specific time frame; and
- Focus on *outcomes* not *outputs*.

An objective should always include the desired outcome, the target audience and a time frame to achieve the objective. A formula or template for writing good objectives is:

To do what with whom by how much within what time frame.

The **Barcelona Principles**—more formally known as the **Barcelona Declaration of Research Principles**—can assist public relations practitioners in developing meaningful objectives.

Developed with the International Association for the Measurement and Evaluation of Communication (AMEC), the Barcelona Principles are a set of seven principles for effective public relations measurement. The principles were adopted at the second annual European Summit on Measurement in Barcelona, Spain in 2010 and are supported by the Global Alliance, the Institute for Public Relations, the International Communications Consultancy Organization, the Public Relations Consultants Association, the Public Relations Society of America, and the Canadian Public Relations Society.

The Barcelona Principles outline the basic principles of PR and communication measurement that are intended to not only demonstrate proof of performance, but how to foster continuous improvement. The Principles are considered foundational in that specific measurement programs with clearly stated goals can be developed from them.

Specifically, the Barcelona Principles identify the importance of goal setting, the need for outcome- instead of output-based measurement of PR campaigns, the importance of excluding ad-value equivalency metrics,[1] the validity of both quantitative and qualitative measurements, the value of social media, and the need for a holistic approach to measurement and evaluation.

AMEC, the founder of the Barcelona Principles, has conducted consultations with AMEC chapters from across the world and has updated the principles over time. The current version, Barcelona 3.0 updated in 2020, is referenced here.

---

1. In other words, the value of earned media coverage should not be calculated as the equivalent of purchasing advertising in print, online, or on television.

The seven principles are as follows:

- **PRINCIPLE 1:** Setting goals is an absolute prerequisite to communications planning, measurement, and evaluation.
- **PRINCIPLE 2:** Measurement and evaluation should identify outputs, outcomes, and potential impact.
- **PRINCIPLE 3:** Outcomes and impact should be identified for stakeholders, society, and the organization.
- **PRINCIPLE 4:** Communication measurement and evaluation should include both qualitative and quantitative analysis.
- **PRINCIPLE 5:** AVEs [ad value equivalencies] are not the value of communication.
- **PRINCIPLE 6:** Holistic communication measurement and evaluation includes all relevant online and offline channels.
- **PRINCIPLE 7:** Communication measurement and evaluation are rooted in integrity and transparency to drive learning and insights.

More information on the Barcelona Principles can be found at: https://amecorg.com/resources/barcelona-principles-3-0/

Objectives address *outcomes* and not *outputs*. We need to change people's perceptions and beliefs **before** we can change their actions. If the city's current residents are aware that the target homeowners for the new development are working people who are just as concerned about safety as they are, they may be more willing to support the project and encourage their municipal councilors to vote to approve it.

An arbitrary metric, such as the level of attendance at an open house, is of much less value. You may have full attendance at a presentation, but it may be because (in this case) residents are angry and oppose your project.

In order to reach the goal of securing approval for the housing development, support from local residents for the project needs to be increased. Baseline research will indicate the current level of support. You will then determine the desired level of increased support that you can realistically obtain.

To gain this support, you would also need an objective that addresses reasons for a lack of support. What do residents know about the project? Is there a need to increase awareness of the project and how it will operate? Again, the baseline research will reveal you the current degrees of awareness and understanding so that you can determine how much of an increase is desired.

It helps to think of objectives as a ladder. What needs to be accomplished before you can move up to the next rung?

Let's return to the example of the BestHomes housing development that we discussed earlier. For this project, the list of objectives might look something like this:

- Increase city residents' awareness of the housing project by 10 percent within three weeks.
- Increase local residents' understanding of the target audience and their need for affordable housing by 40 percent within three weeks.
- Increase support for the project among local residents by 20 percent within two months.

You will see that each step in the "ladder" brings you one rung closer to meeting the goal. Each objective addresses a specific outcome you would like to achieve from a specific public, within a timeframe.

Organizational Objective	Communications Objective	Measurement	Method	Target
Increase confidence	Increase awareness*	% audience who are aware of org	Annual opinion survey	5% increase over baseline scores
	Increase positive sentiment	% audience who express positive sentiment	Annual opinion survey Social media analysis Contact centre calls	10% increase in positive sentiment over baseline

*Our analysis demonstrates that confidence levels are directly correlated to levels of awareness, leading us to conclude that an increase in awareness will support this corporate objective.

Plan Element: Objectives	Research	Measurement
Increase website traffic	Website analytics	% increase awareness
Increase awareness	Pre- and post-campaign surveys	Cost per impression
Increase key messaging resonance	MRP (Media Ratings Points)	
Aligned to Evaluation		

Target Audiences

A **target audience** is a group of people that shares a common interest vis-à-vis an organization, recognizes its significance, and sets out to do something about that interest. A target audience has important characteristics: it is distinguishable, homogeneous, important, large enough to matter, and reachable. Communicating with the right audience is crucial to success. Issues rarely impact one group. The research will help to determine which groups are impacted and how they are impacted. Although the issue may be the same, these various publics may need different messages, and you may have to use different vehicles to reach all audiences.

Examples of Target Audiences

Internal	External
Senior managers	Regulators
Managers	Customers
Supervisors	Competitors
Professional staff	Residents
Technical staff	Business owners
Administrative staff	Special interest groups
Front-line employees	Media
	Relevant levels of government (federal, provincial, regional, municipal)

Each audience will have different information needs and media preferences. It is useful to categorize your audiences to ensure you are focusing your efforts efficiently.

Primary audiences have the ability to impact the organization or are most directly impacted by decisions. They might include board members, management, front-line workers, production staff, IT staff, and shareholders.

Secondary audiences have less ability to directly impact the organization. You will want them to have information as well in order to increase internal understanding and also avoid false perceptions or rumours.

Intervening publics act as gatekeepers for key audiences. Communicators send messages to an intervening public with the expectation that they will pass the message on to the intended audience. The intervening public may be seen as more credible or trustworthy than the source. Individuals in this category may include the news media, supervisors, and support staff.

A **moderating public** includes groups with common goals serving members. A message is communicated to the moderating public to pass on to the intended audience. They may also be seen as more credible or trustworthy than the source; examples include unions and social clubs.

A **traditional audience** is a public with which the organization has a long-standing relationship. An example in the auto industry is "Jeep Nation." This is a group of people loyal to Jeeps and enthusiastic about all they can do and experience with the vehicle. They believe no other vehicle provides the capabilities of a Jeep. Think about the brands you are loyal to, and why you are loyal to them.

A **non-traditional audience** is a public that is unfamiliar to an organization. An example is the ever-growing community of men wearing makeup in South Korea. Men are not a traditional audience for make-up, yet the desire to "put your best face forward" has created an industry worth billions of dollars. Non-traditional audiences can become traditional audiences due to changes in your organization's direction or values, societal values, or changes in personal preference.

Latent audiences are people an organization shares values with, but the connection is not known. For example, an individual might value protection of the environment as does a clothing manufacturer.

A latent audience becomes an **aware public** when an incident occurs that they take interest in because of their values. If a factory owned by clothing manufacturer is found to be damaging a waterway, individuals for whom environmental issues are important become aware of how the company's behaviour misaligns with their values.

An aware public becomes an **active public** when they become engaged in the issue. They might post your thoughts on this incident to social media, write letters to the editor, approach the news media, or participate in demonstrations.

In the case at hand, the clothing manufacturer may communicate how this incident is contrary to their own philosophy and practices and set out what they are doing to ensure it never happens again. With this information, an active public may settle back into becoming an aware public once again.

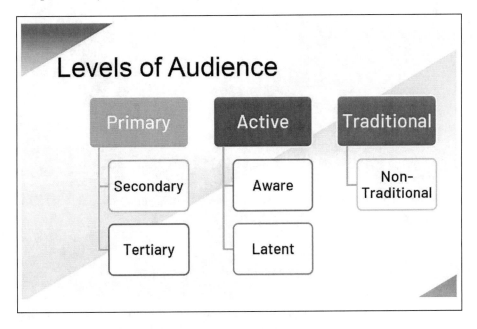

In the context of our example of the proposed low-income housing development, the various publics and audiences might be categorized in this way:

Audience	Audience type(s)
Local residents	Primary Active
Low-income residents in need of housing	Primary Aware
City residents	Secondary Aware Moderating
Social agencies	Primary Active
Current Best Homes owners	Secondary Aware
Potential/Future Best Homes Owners	Tertiary Latent

Key Messages

What Do We Want to Communicate to Our Target Audiences?

To communicate effectively, **key messages** are developed for each audience. A key message can be thought of as the one thing you want the audience to know and remember about your organization and its actions in relation to the issue. Consider each audience carefully—what information does each individual audience need and what information do they want?

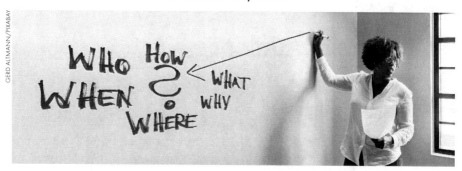

Answer the core questions of who, what, when, where, how and why. This can help guide all of your writing!

- Focus on the facts.
- Try to answer the question WIIFM— "What's in it for me?"

Working through this process, the practitioner can critically examine any issue or opportunity facing an organization. In any given situation, an organization will need to communicate with more than one public.

Each group may require different information, and so it is essential that the PR professional is aware of the different communication needs and preferred medium for each group.

For example, in the context of the BestHomes proposal:

- Local residents will need to know that new residents of the project are all employed. They will also need to know that these future residents share their desire to live in a safe community.
- The potential new residents will need to know how many units are available and the criteria for qualifying to purchase a unit.
- Residents outside of the project community need to know the extent of the affordable housing crisis and the impact this has on members of the community.
- Current owners of BestHomes properties need to know that BestHomes

cares about the community and is helping to provide safe, quality homes for lower-income residents.

Key Characteristics of Key Messages
- Brief statement of most important messages—5 to 20 seconds if read aloud.
- Meaningful, persuasive, interesting.
- Easily understood.
- Explain *why* the information is important.

Key messages are brief statements of your most important messages – five to 20 seconds in length. They must be meaningful and persuasive to the target audience and be interesting to other audiences. They must be easily understood with little room for interpretation or confusion.

Key messages answer questions like:

- Why is this important?
- Why should people care?
- What actions should we take?
- What does this mean in real life?
- What does the average person or specific audience need to know?
- What are the benefits/dangers?
- What specifically is being done or will be accomplished?

Ask yourself as a communicator:

- What is the action I want people to take?
- What is the most important thing about this situation?
- What is the information I have to share?
- What do the public and media need to know?

Support your messages with:

- Evidence
- Statistics
- Understandable examples
- Relevant analogies and metaphors

Message Mapping
Message mapping involves adding data points or backing data to your key message. This data is used to provide evidence and to increase the credibility of

your key message. Returning to the BestHomes scenario, here are some examples of the key message as well as backing statements:

Key message
The proposed BestHomes project will not increase crime in the area.

Backing statement #1 (supporting fact):
The target market for these homes will be working individuals and families.

Backing statement #2:
They are hard-working, dedicated people looking to start their lives in a safe community.

Backing statement #3:
They have just as much desire to live in a safe community as neighbouring residents. As young graduates working their way up in the world, young couples starting families, and new Canadians, personal safety and a sense of home is important to them.

Plan Element: Key Messaging	Research	Measurement
Align particularly with target audiences	Test with focus groups	% increase awareness
	Test with surveys	% increase receptivity

Strategy

How Do We Achieve Our Objectives?

Strategies are the first step in determining how to accomplish objectives. The communication approach should be based on a proactive and/or a reactive strategy.

- **Proactive strategy approach:** enable an organization to launch a communication program under the conditions and according to the timeline that seems to best fit the organization's interests. Examples of proactive strategies: organizational performance (quality of the organization's product or service), audience participation (call to action), alliances and coalitions, sponsorships, influence (advocacy), publicity, newsworthy information (news for the media), transparent communication (dialogue, discussion as equals).
- **Reactive strategy approach:** enable an organization to respond to influences and opportunities from its environment. Examples of reactive strategies: offensive (attack, embarrassment, shock, threat), defensive (denial, excuse, justification), diversionary (concession, ingratiation, disassociation, relabeling), vocal commiseration (concern, condolence, regret, apology), rectifying behavior (investigation, corrective action, restitution, repentance), strategic inaction (silence).

After comparing the advantages and risks of each of the possible strategies stated above, it is important to identify the directions and best strategies, taking into account your communication objectives for each key public.

For example, if you work for a national developer building a new apartment block, you might want to set a proactive strategy approach using a call to action and newsworthy information to engage the local residents and demonstrate the support of local contractors. You will need to develop strategies for *each* target audience.

Some considerations for strategy development include:

- Considering how we will achieve the objective.
- Strategies are the general direction you will take to accomplish the objectives. Strategies identify the best communication approach (proactive, reactive or a mix of both approaches) you will use with a specific communication objective based on that audience's communication needs, preferences, and receptivity.
- Developing strategies for *each* communication objective.

- Listing the best mix of communication approaches to be used.

Strategies related to the BestHome examples could look like this:

- Utilize face-to-face opportunities to engage local residents and inform them of the need for affordable housing projects and create awareness of the intended residents of the project
- Use media relations to communicate the need for affordable housing to residents across the city

Tactics

What Specific Actions Will Get Us to the Objective?

Building from strategies, **tactics** are the activities used to communicate with target audiences.

When it comes to tactics, keep in mind that different audiences may have a preferred method of communication or that one form of communication may be more credible than another.

For example, older people prefer to read a newspaper or watch television than to read news on a smartphone. In an organization, a speech by the CEO is more effective than sending an email.

Focus on the medium most preferred by the audience but use a variety of media to ensure all members of that audience have the opportunity to receive the message.

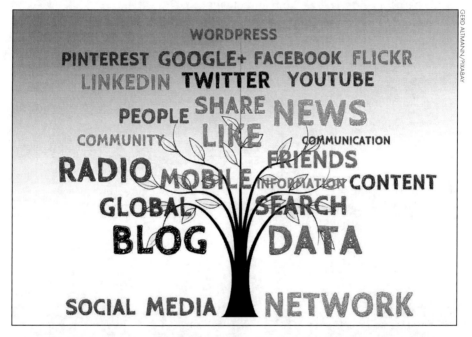

In the plan, describe the tactics that will be used to achieve each strategy. For example:

- Information on a webpage
- Media advisory and/or news release
- Media conference
- Photo op
- Open house

- Town hall
- Print advertising
- Digital advertising
- Newsletter or magazine article
- Brochure
- Posters
- Emails
- Social such as Twitter, Facebook, Instagram, TikTok

Match the media or channel with the specific audience. Be prepared to use more than one vehicle, and keep in mind that each medium has strengths, weaknesses, and relative costs.

Ask these questions:

- What will be done, by whom and at what cost?
- What specific actions will get us to the objective?

Plan Element: Tactics	Research	Measurement
Media relations	MRP	Total impressions, Cost per
Social media	App analytics	Total impressions, Cost per
Website	Website analytics	Total impressions, Cost per
Paid	App analytics, MRP	Total impressions, Cost per
PESO (Paid, Earned, Shared, Owned) universe	Pre- and post-event surveys	Measure outcomes

In the example of the housing development, strategies and associated tactics might be as follows:

Strategy	Tactics
Face-to-face communication	Town Hall
Media relations	Advisory News release News conference Media availability
Digital media	Project specific webpage Social media posts

Timelines/Critical Path

When Are Actions Carried Out?

Be specific and provide soft and hard dates for approvals and all aspects of the plan. For each tactic that needs to be completed:

- Identify the person responsible for completing the task.
- Set out the deadline to complete the task.
- Add a notes column to your tracking spreadsheet or table to keep track of observations and concerns.

The table or spreadsheet need not be complicated to keep you on track:

Task/ Deliverable	Person Responsible	Deadline	Budget	Notes
News release	Jill H.	September 3	N/A	Must be approved by Scott.
Billboard ads	Amy J.	October 4	$10,000	Renew contract for three months

Plan Element: Timelines	Research	Measurement
Align with budget and human capital	Team focus groups	Compare planned to actual

Budget

What Needs to be Spent to Reach the Objective (Both Hard and Soft Costs)?

This is a very important part of the plan. You will need funding in order to create and distribute your tactics.

Be very specific and comprehensive. Include all costs.

Generally, there are a few ways to develop a budget.

In **project-based budgeting**, you are given a set budget that you must stay within. The extent of your tactics is limited by the amount of money available to you. Plans are built to maximize results based on the budget available.

Zero-based budgeting works from the ground up. A budget is built indicating the cost of each tactic. The budget is presented to management or the client, who will either approve it, ask for changes, or trim it down. With zero-based budgeting, it is important to build in some contingencies in case costs increase unexpectedly.

The Fees/Disbursement Model

Fees are calculated on the basis of the number of hours needed per task with an average cost per hour. This model is generally applied to outside consultants. Key actions in developing this kind of budget include:

- Identifying the cost of each tactic.
- Being specific in identifying what must be spent to achieve the objective, both in terms of **hard costs** (money paid to suppliers, outside consultants, or media outlets) and **soft costs** (agency fees or the time-cost equivalencies of internal human capital).
- Human capital must also be included here: Who do we use to do this, and what team do we build? We'll consider this matter in more detail in the next section.

Plan Element: Budget	Research	Measurement
Determine budget limits	Historical, archives	Compare planned to actual
	Accounting	

Human Resources

Who Do We Use to Achieve the Objective? What Team Do We Build?

In allocating human resources to the project, we must consider how many people are needed as well as how many hours will be needed *per task*.

For salaried or contracted employees, it is important to show how much time will be needed to achieve specific tasks.

Be very clear to individuals acting as spokespersons that media work is time-consuming. They must have buy-in from senior management and understand what they have volunteered to do. They must also realize that media requests are extremely time sensitive. Of course, these points will be covered in their media training sessions.

Roles and responsibilities of the team should be clearly spelled out, not just in the timeline, which should capture assignments and due dates, but in a separate section expanding on what the expectations are of each team member.

It is a good idea to consult with the human resources department and legal counsel as this part of the plan is created.

Plan Element: Human Capital	Research	Measurement
Internal teams	Media training to determine best spokespersons	Credibility
External teams	Availability	Performance
Back-ups determined		

Evaluation

Why Is It So Important to Evaluate the Outcomes of a Project?

Evaluation is important for two reasons. Firstly, it is crucial to conduct an on-going critical examination of a project's communication goals and objectives and their success, and to pinpoint where the project has not achieved its full potential. Secondly, the impact of a communication initiative (its **outcomes**) has to be evaluated during the active phase and at the end. Evaluation can prevent expensive errors, suggest alternative strategies and improve the effectiveness of the message.

Evaluation of outcomes must be tied directly to the project's objectives to determine if you accomplished what you set out to achieve. Here are some examples of questions that a communicator should keep in mind:

- Were the project's objectives met?
- How will the objectives be measured?
- Did we do what we set out to do?
- How did the organization's management and other publics view this project?
- Did we meet the client's needs and expectations?

It's important to measure objectives *before* measuring other metrics, such as additional relevant outputs. Always show how you will evaluate your objectives first. Tie the evaluation of the project directly to the objectives.

When carrying out post-communication research with a view to comparing what we learned before the communications activity with how things stand afterward, a similar method using similar questions should be used. We would want to ask the same questions of members of the same public—though not necessarily the exact same individuals. This will reveal any increase in awareness.

Focus on the outcomes—the changes in behaviour, knowledge, and perception that lead to a change in action. You may include outputs such as the number of positive letters to the editor or "likes" on social media, but be sure to measure the right things the right way.

The client's assessment of the project can also be part of the evaluation. This can serve as a testimonial as well in searching for new work and clients in the future.

Also, it is good PR practice to add your own post mortem analysis, discussing the lessons learned and recommendations to take into account when carrying out similar work in the future.

Here are some examples of evaluation activities that take place during the implementation of a communication project:

- Testing of the communication concept and key messages.
- Decisions related to communication tactics and budget.
- Gauging the reactions of senior management, stakeholders, and other publics.

Once a project has been completed, evaluation activities may include assessment of its outcomes as well as other effects linked to the communication activities (for instance, advertising, social media, media coverage, etc.). The number of calls for action for an initiative or purchases of a product or a service may also be measured in order to evaluate the success of a project. The reactions of senior management and stakeholders may also be factors to consider.

Media Rating Points ("MRP") are another important tool to measure a communications campaign's effectiveness. This kind of content analysis can track various kinds of media coverage and can also be helpful in measuring media reaction to crisis communications activities or gauging the influence of media attention in unplanned and unanticipated situations (whether good or bad). Using this system allows insight into both a campaign's **total reach** (the total number of people a campaign reaches) and **cost per contact** (how much money it costs to reach each individual).

Plan Element: Evaluation	Research	Measurement
Aligned with objectives	Outputs – MRP/other analytics	MRP and website and app analytics
	Outcomes	% increase awareness, behaviour change, sales
	Pre- and post-campaign surveys	

Keep in mind that the objectives for a project are written in response to the results of the baseline research. These objectives are set to help meet the overall goal, and so they take precedence for evaluation.

A plan is written prior to a project getting underway. In other words, when a plan is written you have not yet communicated your messages. In a plan, therefore, this section provides information on how you intend to evaluate whether you met your objectives. For the BestHomes scenario, the plan might look like this:

Objective 1

Increase city resident awareness of the housing project by 10 per cent within three weeks.

Evaluation: Resurvey a sample of city residents to determine the level of awareness of the project at the end of the campaign.

Objective 2

Increase local residents understanding of the target audience and their need for affordable housing by 40 per cent within three weeks.

Evaluation: Resurvey a sample of local residents to determine the level of understanding of the need for affordable housing at the end of the campaign.

Objective 3

Increase support for project with local residents by 20 per cent within two months.

Evaluation: Resurvey a sample of local residents to determine if the level of support for the project has increased at the end of the campaign.

Evaluating Outputs

There may be other metrics that are useful when demonstrating the success of a campaign, such as attendance at an open house, media coverage or the degree of social media interaction.

When using these outputs, it is important to provide context around these numbers. An open house may be very well attended, but maybe it is because those attending want to express their opposition to the project. To get a true picture of the level of support attendees could fill out a questionnaire at the end of the meeting.

Tracking media coverage can provide a sense of how the public will perceive the issue. The number of news articles and the placement of the articles (close to the front page or first in the televised lineup) demonstrates that the issue is seen as important. But we must pay attention to:

- The tone of the articles—was it positive or negative?
- Balance—were opposing views included in the coverage?
- Key messages—were they included in the coverage?
- Spokesperson effectiveness—was our spokesperson credible?
- Reader/viewer comments—if available, what was the number and nature of public comments on the coverage?

Case Studies

Once a communications plan has been successfully completed, it can be written up as a **case study**. A case study is written in the past tense (since the events it describes have already happened). It includes the results and actual costs of the campaign, an assessment by the client or senior management, and a post mortem analysis by the communications professional who carried out the campaign.

If a campaign is particularly noteworthy, it can serve as the basis for an award entry. And a case study conveniently gathers together in one place important material that may be helpful in future projects as well as in assisting an organization in its goal of continuous improvement. Insights drawn from such case studies may also be helping in securing new business for an organization and in making new employees familiar with past successes.

The following section presents some case studies that, of course, originally started out as plans.

Case Study
Yellow Brick House Pathway for Peace

Background
- Yellow Brick House is a non-profit shelter for abused women and children and homeless women and children, serving York Region (north of Toronto).
- United Way funding had been cut drastically, so the shelter was dependent on the Ministry of Community and Social Services (COMSOC) for most of its funding.
- It had to generate about $300,000 per year in self-raised funds to meet its current budget.

Goals
- To create a sustainable fundraising mechanism for the shelter as well as provide a location for ongoing public events since the shelter itself is a highly secure facility.
- To provide a venue for raising awareness about abuse of women and children.

Objectives
- Generate awareness of Yellow Brick House and issues such as abuse and homelessness through media coverage.
- Generate money through brick sales.

Audiences
- York Region-based families and businesses.
- Stakeholders such as COMSOC and shelter staff (members of CUPE).
- Those suffering or who have suffered abuse.
- Politicians, including local, regional, provincial and federal.

Messages
- Abuse against women and children is an underreported and serious societal issue.
- We are building this public pathway to raise money and awareness of the issue, as well as provide a place for solace and mourning and the holding of public events.
- This shelter needed community financial help to stay open.

Strategy
- Attract a noted celebrity to open the pathway so it can raise money and awareness at the same time.
- Fix it in time and space.

Tactics: Create a Venue
- The project was designed to refurbish a rundown public space.
- Through that space, a pathway of cobblestones was built and a monument erected. Then the cobblestones or "bricks" were "sold" in kind.
- Plaques (several of them over the project's five-year time frame) were erected honouring those who "bought" bricks. News media and other key stakeholders were invited to those events.

Tactics: Launch Event
- A media advisory was distributed via paid wire and email one week prior to events.
- Videographer was hired at half-rate for launch event where he shot professional-quality video. Dubbed at downtown facility and delivered by driver to all GTA TV outlets.
- Photographer shot images on professional digital camera at all three events. Emailed to key local media each time.

Timelines/Critical Path
- Teaser photo-op event of monument arrival for engraving held on May 23, 2000.
- Launch event held on June 27, 2000 with the Honourable Hilary M. Weston and Aurora Mayor Tim Jones in attendance. Invitees to launch included key COMSOC officials, other local politicians, more than 100 school children and dozens of Yellow Brick House staff, volunteer board members and former residents. Ribbon cutting/plaque unveiling conducted by Weston and Jones.
- Plaque commemoration events were held September 26, 2000 and June 29, 2001 where plaques were unveiled on the monument. Mayor Jones attended both.

Budget
- Fees: public relations counsel and project management was pro bono.
- Disbursements: $32,860 including landscaping and pathway construction, three monument stones, engraving and placement, three sets of plaques.

Evaluation

- More than 30 million total impressions were generated in news media over five-year period including local TV outlets such as CKVR-TV (now CTV2 Barrie), Shaw and Rogers, local newspapers such as the Era Banner, Town Crier, the Liberal and the Auroran, Global TV, and CBC Radio (which aired a five-minute documentary).
- The path paid for itself in six months. It so far has raised about $4,000 in profits that go directly into shelter revenues.

Results

- Considerable interest was generated around the world in the concept.
- This led to our dream of creating an international network of pathways of peace.
- We formed a separate organization to build other pathways, with one in Scarborough in process.
- A labour dispute a year later at this particular shelter led to its demise—but the Pathway still stands!

Case Study
CrosSled
(Winner, CPRS Toronto ACE Awards: Bronze, Special Events, 2002)

Background
- CrosSled's annual sales growth rate of 50 percent per year over four seasons was based largely on awareness generated by media relations and print advertising.
- The total communications budget was approximately $30,000, which included targeted media buys.
- The Kortright Centre had come to CrosSled in its second season wanting to use the product as part of their public participation program.
- About six CrosSleds ended up being used quite successfully during the 1999/2000 season.

Research
- CrosSled customers were asking about a community event—they wanted to meet others in the CrosSled community.
- We looked into the idea of community events like those organized by the Saturn auto brand, which included free drive-in movies for Saturn drivers.

Assessment
- In the 2000/2001 season planning, PR counsel recommended that a grassroots style public event was needed to publicize the CrosSled product and sport.
- We approached Kortright in our third season in order to partner with them to hold the "CrosSled Rendezvous."

Assessment: Venue Selection
- Kortright Centre, Sunday, January 14, 2001, 11:00 a.m. to 2:00 p.m.

Goals
- To continue growing our brand and sport.
- To build brand equity among current customers and potential ones.
- To generate word-of-mouth through event attendees.

Objectives
- To generate awareness through measurable media coverage.
- To measure the number of attendees at the event.

Audiences
- Current CrosSled customers (via direct invite).
- Kortright newsletter recipients (via Kortright newsletter distribution).
- General winter enthusiasts (Korthright visitors).

Messages
- CrosSled, an ancient Scandinavian winter conveyance device, is perfectly suited for Canadian winter usage.
- It is fun, easy and affordable.
- It is the Swiss Army knife of sleds suitable for serious winter athletes, casual users, use as a winter stroller, even as an affordable dog sled.

Strategy
- Provide a fun-filled environment to stimulate grassroots enthusiasm and word-of-mouth endorsement for the product among current and potential customers.

Strategic Considerations
- Venue must offer outdoor winter amenities as well as indoor facilities.
- Venue must be known to media and easily accessible to media.
- Venue must be a central point for all GTA customers.

Tactics: Event Elements
- Hard-packed trail for relay race, more serious race, and kids' scavenger hunt (for marshmallows).
- About a dozen sleds available for free demo, including handful of the new Racers.
- BBQ for cookout (hot dogs, hamburgers, soft drinks, beer).
- Music available (ABBA) via portable CD player.
- Hired videographer to shoot video.
- Prizes for event winners (CrosSled hats and scarves).
- CrosSled maintenance clinic.
- Invited CrosSled partners (i.e., Wil Wegman, Canadian Ice Fishing Team).

Tactics: Media Relations
- Media advisory distributed via CNW one week prior (January 5) with repeats on the Friday and Saturday mornings. Media advisory also distributed directly via email to comprehensive media list.
- Videographer shot professional-quality video. Dubbed in field. Delivered by driver to all GTA TV outlets.

- Photographer shot on professional digital camera. Emailed to paid wire service from field.

Timelines/Critical Path
- Planning commenced three months from event.
- Involved Kortright as partner and utilized its relationships to promote the event.
- Date selected for ideal snow coverage.
- Media advisory out a week prior, and repeated day before and day of event.

Budget
- Fees: $3,375.
- Disbursements: $5,775.
- Total: $9,150.

Evaluation
- Number of attendees at event and quality and quantity of media coverage generated.
- About 100 people attended, 20 of whom were current customers!

Evaluation: Attending Media
- City-tv
- Toronto Star
- TVOntario (documentary team)
- Liberal (York Region Newspaper Group)

Evaluation: Media Coverage
- More than 6.1 million impressions.
- Pre-event coverage on 680 News, and event coverage on City-tv and TVOntario (eight-minute documentary repeated several times during the 2001 and 2002 seasons).

Evaluation: Media Assets
- The photograph and caption distributed by the paid news wire was picked up by the Liberal, Sault Star and King Sentinel.
- Pick-up of our B-roll footage of the event on CFTO-TV (CTV Toronto) and Global TV.

Post Mortem
- We needed sleds to be pre-assembled.

- We needed more human capital to cook hamburgers and hot dogs.
- We needed sales and PR backup on site.
- This would allow client and PR counsel to handle media better since the TVO crew overwhelmed us with their unanticipated needs.
- These human capital needs were applied to the successful 2002 Rendez-vous, on held January 27, 2002.

The Product's Fate
- The product lasted five seasons.
- Lack of retail outlets did not help our "scratch and sniff" cultural need in Canada at that time to shop in person.
- Running an online-only business proved ahead of its time.
- The manufacturer in Norway restructured so we lost the option of free shipping to Canada.
- Winters continued to be very mild with lots of news about global warming and limited amounts of snow, both of which hurt sales.

Case Study
Canadian Canoe Pilgrimage 2017

Background

In 1967, 24 Jesuits paddled in canoes from Martyrs' Shrine near Midland, Ontario to Expo 67 in Montreal, a distance of 850 kilometres as measured on a map. It took 21 days. Fifty years later, a core group of 30 paddlers (about one-third Jesuits, one-third Indigenous people, and one-third lay collaborators), successfully completed the same journey in July and August 2017, this time continuing the work of the Truth and Reconciliation Commission as well as celebrating Canada's 150th birthday. The 2017 journey took a total of 25 days.

Mission Statement: "Paddling Together"

The Canadian Canoe Pilgrimage brought together different cultures that form the fabric of Canada today. The pilgrimage was designed to provide an experience of encounter that would encourage dialogue, reconciliation and friendship. Participants were immersed in the Calls-to-Action outlined by the Truth and Reconciliation Commission. Our vehicle for this encounter was a canoe pilgrimage spanning 25 days and 850 kilometres along a traditional water trade route with paddlers from Indigenous communities, Jesuits, English and French Canadians, men and women, young and old.

Goals

- Continuing the work of Canada's Truth and Reconciliation Commission (TRC) by fostering a community of paddlers comprised of Indigenous Peoples, Jesuits, English and French Canadians, young and old, male and female;
- Fundraising for the Canadian Canoe Pilgrimage (CCP) as well as for apostolates of the Jesuits in English Canada;
- Raising awareness of the Jesuits' significant role in the founding of Canada; and
- Increasing awareness of the Jesuits for those discerning a vocation either to religious life or in support one of the Jesuits' apostolates in Canada.

Objectives

- Through proactive media relations, generate positive media coverage in both the consumer and food trade news holes to help drive awareness and sales. At least 10 million total impressions will be generated, utilizing the MRP measurement system with a cost per contact of $0.05 or less.

Target Audiences: Media

- Internet news providers via paid wire distribution.
- Community newspapers and radio and TV stations along the route.
- Mayors, MPPs, and MPs were sent letters and media advisories relevant to route.
- National media, such as the CBC.
- Facebook, with less focus on Twitter and Instagram.
- Jesuit- and Catholic-oriented media.

Target Audiences: Stakeholders

- The Jesuits in English and French Canada, as well as Jesuits within the Canada–US Jesuit Conference.
- Indigenous peoples of Canada.
- Local parishes along the route.
- Young adults.
- Federal, provincial, regional and municipal governments.
- Media partners.

Key Messages/Primary Messaging

1. To bring different cultures together…

Canada is a mosaic. We are at our best when we celebrate and encourage diversity as well as grow in our understanding and appreciation of different cultures and traditions. Simply being with members of other cultures and traditions and experiencing things together fuels this learning.

2. To encourage the skills needed for dialogue, reconciliation, and relationship building…

Our society is becoming increasingly polarized. The skills need to combat this division are dialogue and active listening, trusting and respecting the other's viewpoint, and developing the capacity to share our own vulnerabilities.

3. To increase awareness around Canada's Truth and Reconciliation Commission and its Calls-to-Action…

The TRC's Calls-to-Action require immediate and active participation in order to acknowledge past and change current injustices faced by the Indigenous peoples in Canada. It is this active participation that leads to trust and relationship building which are necessary for reconciliation.

4. To build on our rich and varied traditions…

Our various traditions are rich sources of wisdom. We must better understand these teachings of our ancestors in order that their richness can be shared for generations to come.

5. To foster a deeper respect, immersion and connection with all of creation around us…

We are living in an ecological crisis. Scientists and some government leaders are stressing the need for immediate change. Pope Francis and other leaders, in solidarity with Indigenous peoples (who have always valued living in harmony with creation), stress the urgency for personal and communal conversion.

Strategy

- Utilized the local media angle of the pilgrimage moving through various locations to build a national story as well as springboard key messaging per the continuation of the Truth and Reconciliation Commission's Calls-to-Action.

Tactics: Media Plan

- Paid wire (Meltwater) was utilized for the initial news release three months prior to launch and for the launch media advisory.
- Media advisories were distributed in advance of each major media event including those for the French River landing, and for events in North Bay, Mattawa, Pembroke, Ottawa, and Montreal.
- Social media was utilized, including a Facebook page, Twitter and Instagram feeds.
- A wrap-up news release was distributed upon the successful final landing at Kahnawà:ke.
- Embedded videography and photography with the entire trip, which was heavily utilized by media for stories, with a vast amount of imaging collected for a post-trip documentary.

Timelines

- Planning and development began two years prior to the launch on July 21; Ontario Government grant was received approximately one year prior to launch, making the event viable; canoes were rented or borrowed for 30 days.
- Midland/Barrie/Orillia: Launch Mass and event, Saint Marie Park, July 21.
- French River/Sudbury/North Bay: Special event at French River Visitor's Centre, July 28.
- North Bay—Special event at Sisters of St. Joseph Motherhouse, July 31.
- Mattawa—Special dinner at St. Anne's Parish, August 2.
- Pembroke—Special event at Sisters of St. Joseph, August 6.
- Ottawa—Special event at Royal Ottawa Golf Club, August 10.
- Montreal—Special landing event at Villa St. Martin, August 14.
- Kahnawà:ke—Final landing, August 15.

PR Budget

- Total Fees: $59,325.
- Total Disbursements: $7,700.
- Total Fees/Disbursements: $67,025.
- Total PR Hours: 900.

Human Capital

- Mark Hunter LaVigne, MA, APR, FCPRS (PR Director, Agency/Consultant)
- Erica Zlomislic (Communications Officer, Jesuits English Canada)
- Adam Pittman, SJ (PR Logistics Embedded)

- Marco Veilleux (Communications Officer, Jesuits French Canada, Montreal Event)

Spokespersons:
- Erik Sorensen, SJ (Key Jesuit and trip spokesperson, Trip Director)
- Kevin Kelly, SJ (Back-up Spokesperson, Coordinator, Logistics and fundraising)
- Paul Jacques (Embedded Navigator, Indigenous Spokesperson)

Videography/Photography:
- Tim Wilson (Director)
- Eric Miller (Embedded videography)
- Dominik Haake (Embedded photography)

PR Advisers:
- Ian Ross, APR
- Daniel Granger, LLB, MBA, APR, FCPRS
- Pierrette Leonard, APR, FCPRS

Evaluation
- Total impressions: 43,546,773
- Total stories: 180
- Total stories, English: 137
- Total stories, French: 43
- Total stories, print/online: 86
- Total stories, broadcast: 94
- Total fees: $59,325
- Total disbursements: $7,700
- Total cost per impression: $0.0015
- MRP Score: 90.81 %

Evaluation: Media Results
- 11-minute documentary on CBC-TV's *The National* on Labour Day, 2017 (https://www.cbc.ca/player/play/1039382083875)
- Coverage on APTN *National News*

Front Pages:
- Midland Mirror
- Orillia Packet Times
- North Bay Nugget

- Pembroke Daily Observer
- Radio-Canada Montreal, Moncton, Winnipeg
- Catholic Register and catholicregister.ca
- PrairieMessenger.ca (Indigenous)
- Windspeaker (Indigenous)
- Crc-Canada.org
- Ignatiansolidarity.ca
- Canadianyachting.ca
- CKAT North Bay
- Prescence-info.ca (Cathiolic news service in French)
- Radio VM and radiovm.com (Catholic radio network in Quebec)
- KFM Radio
- Mywestnippissingnow.com
- Mattawa Recorder
- Bonnyville Nouvelle
- La Voix du Nord
- Simcoe.com
- Radio-Canada (Extensively)
- CTV Barrie and barriectvnews.ca
- RDI Matin
- Baytoday.ca
- La Presse
- Plus.lapresse.ca
- Sudbury Star and thesudburystar.ca
- Aptnnews.ca
- CKSH Sherbrooke
- Ottawa Sun and ottawasun.com
- CBC Ontario Morning
- CBC.ca
- CBC Radio North, Sudbury, Windsor, Quebec
- CTV Sudbury, North Bay, Ottawa
- Radio VM Montreal, Victoriaville, Trois Rivieres, Sherbrooke, Rimouski
- CTV Ottawa
- CBC Radio Ottawa
- CBC Radio Montreal
- CBC-TV Montreal, Edmonton, Calgary, Regina

Acknowledgments

The authors wish to thank the following individuals for their assistance in preparing this book:

- David Stover, for supporting us in these multiple PR textbooks and helping us add to the body of knowledge in the profession;
- Daniel Granger for his unwavering support and for writing such great forewords to the books;
- Kim Blanchette, APR, Chart.PR (CIPR), FCPRS and Colleen Killingworth, MCM, APR, FCPRS for their input on how this book fits into the RACE formula;
- Our peer reviewers William Wray Carney, Anne Marie Males, MCM, APR, and Marc Angers, MA, APR, FCPRS.

Recommended Reading

Balloffet, Pierre, George E. Belch, Michael A. Belch, Michael A. Guolla, and François Coderre. *Communication marketing: une perspective intégrée* (3e éd.). Chenelière Éducation, 2013.

Carney, William Wray, and Leah-Anne Lymer. *Fundamentals of Public Relations and Marketing Communications.* University of Alberta Press, 2015.

Carney, William Wray, Colin Babiuk, and Mark Hunter LaVigne. *In the News* (3rd ed.). University of Alberta Press, 2019.

LaVigne, Mark Hunter, Colin Babiuk, and Buddy Jarjoura. *Internal Communications in Canada.* Rock's Mills Press, 2022.

Paine, Katie Delahaye. *Measure What Matters: Online Tools f*

or Understanding Customers, Social Media, Engagement, and Key Relationships. Wiley, 2011.

Smith, Ronald D. (2005). *Strategic Planning for Public Relations* (6th ed.). Taylor and Francis, 2020.

About the Authors

Mark Hunter LaVigne, MA, APR, FCPRS, LM, knows both sides of the "media fence," having worked as a journalist and, since 1990, in a variety of roles in public relations including major agencies, his own practice for a quarter-century and teaching public relations in a number of colleges and universities, most recently in the BPR programs at Humber and Centennial Colleges.

Colin Babiuk, MA, APR, FCPRS is an Associate Professor at MacEwan University in Edmonton. He has over 30 years of experience as a PR practitioner including extensive work in issues management, stakeholder relations and media relations.

Kim Blanchette, APR, Chart. PR (CIPR), FCPRS has more than 30 years of experience in strategic communications, engagement, brand and reputation management, and crisis communications and media relations at the provincial, federal, and international levels, with a focus on public sector and regulatory bodies.

Colleen Killingsworth, MCM, APR, FCPRS has more than 30 years of experience in management consulting, change management and strategic communications. She has a strong track record in leadership, collaboration, successfully managing complex, transformational projects and quickly earning the confidence and support of internal and external stakeholders.